# Squares

Teddy Borth

Abdo
SHAPES ARE FUN!
Kids

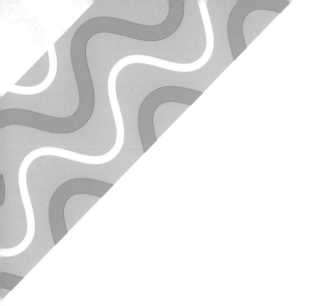

**abdopublishing.com**

Published by Abdo Kids, a division of ABDO, PO Box 398166, Minneapolis, Minnesota 55439.
Copyright © 2016 by Abdo Consulting Group, Inc. International copyrights reserved in all countries.
No part of this book may be reproduced in any form without written permission from the publisher.

Printed in the United States of America, North Mankato, Minnesota.

102015

012016

THIS BOOK CONTAINS
RECYCLED MATERIALS

Photo Credits: iStock, Shutterstock

Production Contributors: Teddy Borth, Jennie Forsberg, Grace Hansen

Design Contributors: Candice Keimig, Dorothy Toth

Library of Congress Control Number: 2015941980

Cataloging-in-Publication Data

Borth, Teddy.
 Squares / Teddy Borth.
   p. cm. -- (Shapes are fun!)
ISBN 978-1-68080-146-0 (lib. bdg.)
Includes index.
1. Squares--Juvenile literature.  2. Geometry--Juvenile literature.  3. Shapes--Juvenile literature.   I. Title.
516/.154--dc23
                        2015941980

# Table of Contents

# Squares

A square has 4 sides.

Each side is the same length.

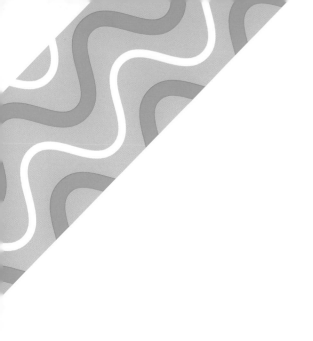

This shape is found all over!

They are on signs.

They tell us what to do.

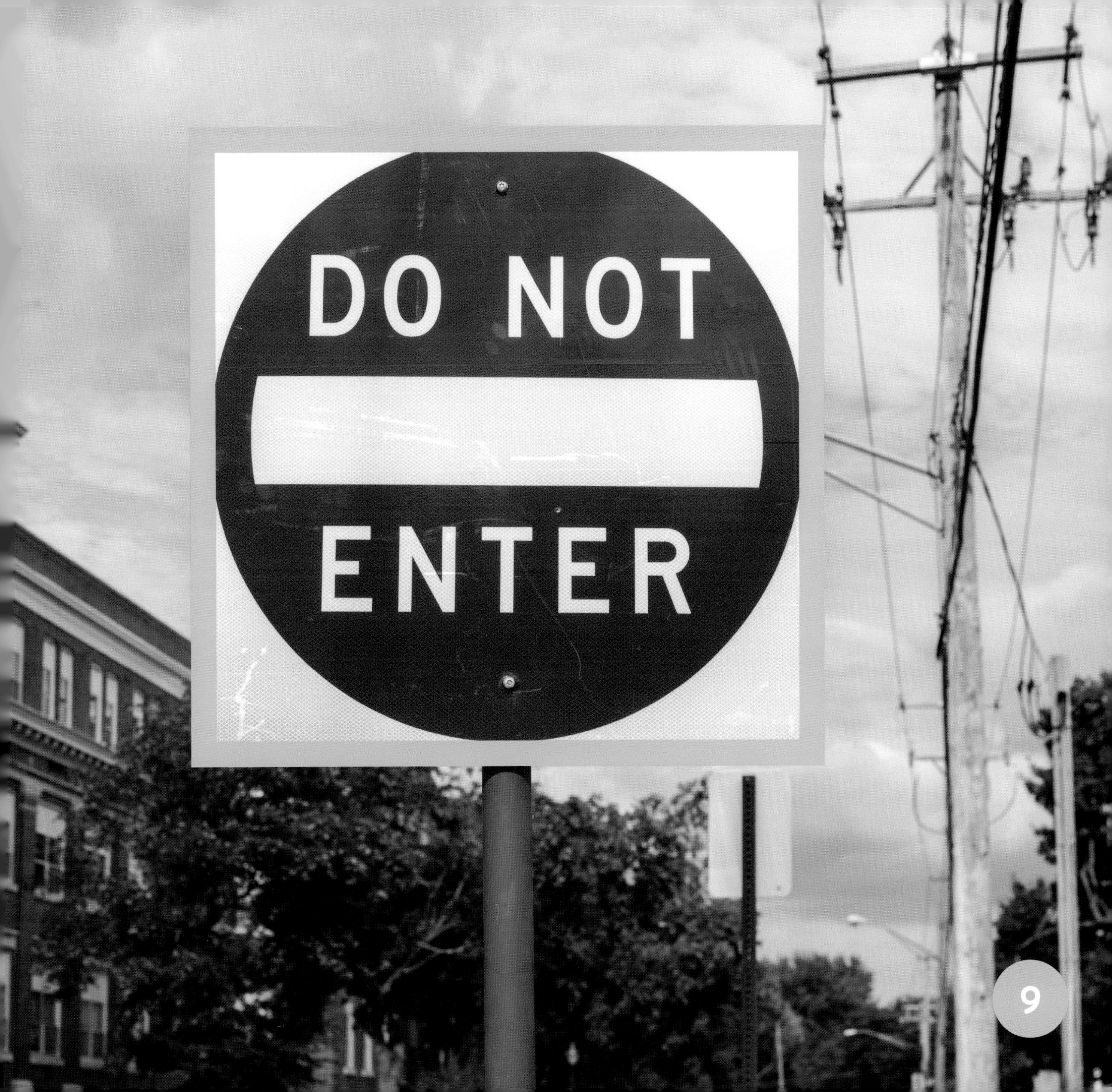
DO NOT
ENTER

They are on floors.

The tiles fit together easily.

They are on waffles.

Hannah eats them!

They are on clothes.

Joe wears a **checkered** shirt.

They are on screens.

They make a picture.

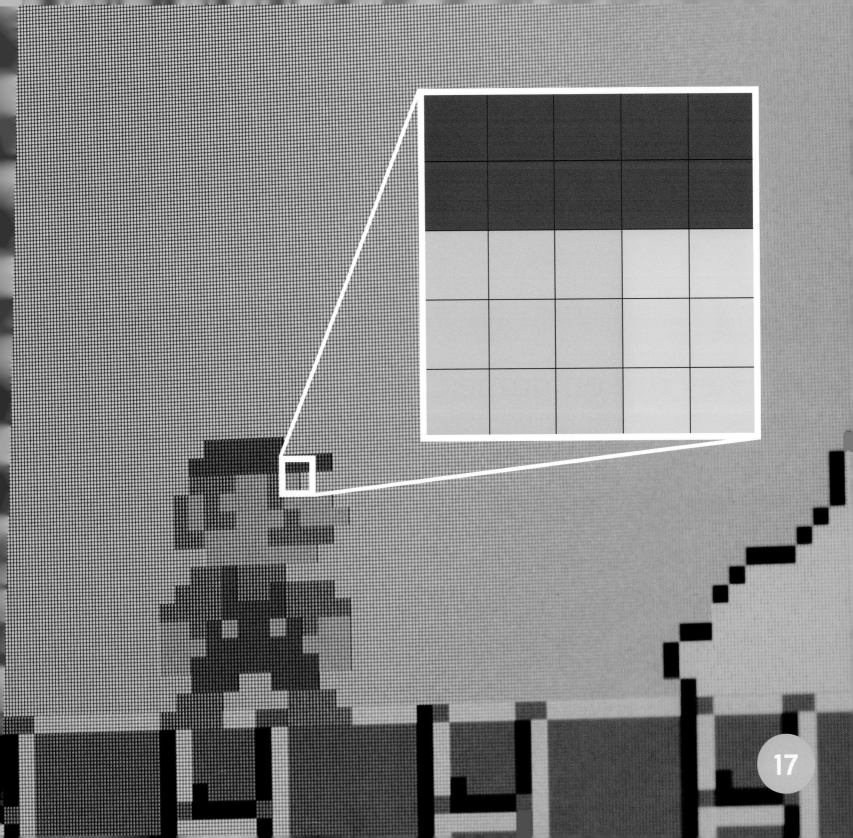

They are on games.

They show us where to move.

Look around you!

You will find a square.

# Count the Squares!

# Glossary

**checkered**
having a pattern made up
of squares.

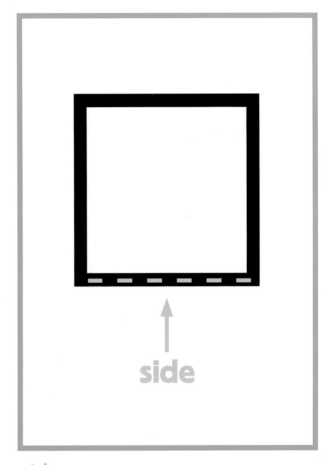

**side**
a line forming a border of
an object.

# Index

## abdokids.com

Use this code to log on to abdokids.com and access crafts, games, videos, and more!

Abdo Kids Code:
# SSK1460